Natural and Everyday Drugs
A False Sense of Security

ILLICIT AND MISUSED DRUGS

ILLICIT AND MISUSED DRUGS

Natural and Everyday Drugs
A False Sense of Security

by Ida Walker

Mason Crest

Mason Crest
370 Reed Road
Broomall, Pennsylvania 19008
www.masoncrest.com

Printed in the Hashemite Kingdom of Jordan.

First printing
9 8 7 6 5 4 3 2 1

Library of Congress Cataloging-in-Publication Data

Walker, Ida.
Natural and everyday drugs : a false sense of security / Ida Walker.
      p. cm.
Includes bibliographical references and index.
ISBN 978-1-4222-2437-3 (hardcover)
ISBN 978-1-4222-2424-3 (series hardcover)
ISBN 978-1-4222-9301-0 (ebook)
1. Drug abuse—Juvenile literature. 2. Drugs, Nonprescription—
Juvenile literature. 3. Caffeine—Juvenile literature. I. Title.
  HV5809.5.W355 2012
  613.8—dc23
                                        2011032583

Interior design by Benjamin Stewart.
Cover design by Torque Advertising + Design.
Produced by Harding House Publishing Services, Inc.
www.hardinghousepages.com

CONTENTS

INTRODUCTION

Addicting drugs are among the greatest challenges to health, well-being, and the sense of independence and freedom for which we all strive—and yet these drugs are present in the everyday lives of most people. Almost every home has alcohol or tobacco waiting to be used, and has medicine cabinets stocked with possibly outdated but still potentially deadly drugs. Almost everyone has a friend or loved one with an addiction-related problem. Almost everyone seems to have a solution neatly summarized by word or phrase: medicalization, legalization, criminalization, war-on-drugs.

For better and for worse, drug information seems to be everywhere, but what information sources can you trust? How do you separate misinformation (whether deliberate or born of ignorance and prejudice) from the facts? Are prescription drugs safer than "street" drugs? Is occasional drug use really harmful? Is cigarette smoking more addictive than heroin? Is marijuana safer than alcohol? Are the harms caused by drug use limited to the users? Can some people become addicted following just a few exposures? Is treatment or counseling just for those with serious addiction problems?

These are just a few of the many questions addressed in this series. It is an empowering series because it provides the information and perspectives that can help people come to their own opinions and find answers to the challenges posed by drugs in their own lives. The series also provides further resources for information and assistance, recognizing that no single source has all the answers. It should be of interest and relevance to areas of study spanning biology, chemistry, history, health, social studies and more. Its efforts to provide a real-world context for the information that is clearly presented but not overly simplified should be appreciated by students, teachers, and parents.

The series is especially commendable in that it does not pretend to pose easy answers or imply that all decisions can be made on the basis of simple facts: some challenges have no immediate or simple solutions, and some solutions will need to rely as much upon basic values as basic facts. Despite this, the series should help to at least provide a foundation of knowledge. In the end, it may help as much by pointing out where the solutions are not simple, obvious, or known to work. In fact, at many points, the reader is challenged to think for him- or herself by being asked what his or her opinion is.

A core concept of the series is to recognize that we will never have all the facts, and many of the decisions will never be easy. Hopefully, however, armed with information, perspective, and resources, readers will be better prepared for taking on the challenges posed by addictive drugs in everyday life.

— *Jack E. Henningfield, Ph.D.*

7 What Are Natural and Everyday Drugs?

You've seen the ads:

"Never diet again! Our all-natural treatment magically melts away the pounds!"

"Want to boost your athletic performance? Dr. Smith has found the secret to improved stamina and strength with his all-natural formula!"

"Need more energy? Our all-natural juice product will give you the pick-me-up you need!"

"Want to increase your bust line?"

"Make your hair thicker?"

"Slim your thighs?"

"Be more alert?"

"Be smarter, stronger, thinner, more beautiful?"

"Then take this amazing, all-natural, brand-new, wonder product!"

After all, what do you have to lose? If it's all natural, it can't hurt. Or can it?

If you have trouble believing these ads, you're right to be skeptical. "All-natural" dietary supplements seldom deliver the amazing results they claim. And just because they're natural, doesn't mean that some of these substances can't cause serious damage to a user's health. After

The phrase "all-natural" may make diet supplements and products sound appealing, but it does not mean they are safe. For example, the foxglove plant contains an "all-natural," and very deadly, poison called digitalis.

What's a Drug?

According to the scientific community, a drug is a chemical substance that affects how the body works; when not abused, it is useful in the diagnosis, treatment, or prevention of a disease or as a component of a medication.

all, plenty of poisonous substances—from apple seeds to hemlock, nightshade to foxglove—are completely natural—and deadly!

But if something is for sale, then it must be safe. The makers of these products wouldn't be able to make their claims if they weren't true. Right?

Wrong.

"Natural" Substances and the Government

In the United States, the Food and Drug Administration (FDA) has strict regulations that govern medicines and the claims that can be made about them. In Canada, an agency called the Therapeutic Product Directorate (TPD), a part of Health Canada, has similar functions. These agencies regulate if, and how medicinal products enter the market in Canada and the United States.

Operating under the authority given it by the government, and guided by laws established throughout the twentieth century, the FDA has established a rigorous drug approval process that verifies the safety, effectiveness, and accuracy of labeling for any drug marketed in the United States. But the type of products that advertise themselves as "all-natural" are usually not considered medicines. Instead, they are "food supplements," which means they are governed by a completely different set of regulations.

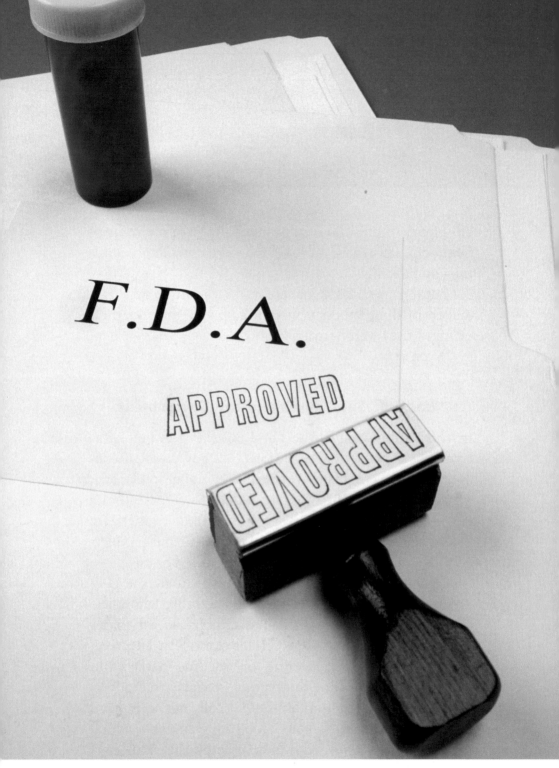

Prescription drugs are required to go through rigorous testing before they are approved by the FDA. However, herbal remedies and supplements are not tested by the FDA prior to being sold.

How Do Dietary Supplements Enter the Market?

If a manufacturer hopes to sell a product as a dietary supplement that contains a "new dietary ingredient," then it must do certain things first, in order to ensure a relationship with the FDA that will free the manufacturer from the requirements imposed on substances labeled as drugs. At least 75 days before being introduced or delivered for introduction into interstate commerce, the manufacturer or distributor of the dietary ingredient or dietary supplement has to provide the FDA with information about the substance, including any citation in published articles, which is the basis on which the manufacturer or distributor has concluded that a dietary supplement containing such dietary ingredient can reasonably be expected to be safe.

Under the Dietary Supplement Health and Education Act of 1994 (DSHEA), the manufacturer itself is responsible for ensuring that a dietary supplement is safe before it is marketed. The FDA is responsible for taking action against any unsafe dietary supplement product *after* it reaches the market. Pharmaceutical companies must go through strict procedures that involve years of tests before the FDA will give its approval to their products—but manufacturers of dietary supplements do not need to register with the FDA nor get FDA approval before producing or selling their products.

DSHEA opened the floodgates for consumers to be bombarded with "supplements" for every ailment and human condition. Essentially, DSHEA created a new category of health claims, referred to as "structure or function" claims. Under DSHEA, products could be labeled with claims that they enhance, improve, or support a biological structure or function without any FDA oversight. For example, a company could claim that its

Some dietary supplements contain chitin, the substance found in the exo-skeleton of shrimp and other shellfish. Chitin claims to block fat from being absorbed.

Weight-Loss the Natural Way

Some of the most popular dietary supplements on the market today advertise that they can cause miraculous weight loss. These supplements claim to
use a variety of methods to back their claims. Their effectiveness, however,
has not been proven with scientific studies. Here are some of the more common ingredients and their reported weight-loss mechanisms:

- Caffeine, guarana, and country mallow claim to increase metabolism.
- Guar gum, glucomannan, and psyllium claim to cause a "full" feeling.
- Hydrocitric acid, green tea, conjugated linoleic acid, and pyruvate claim to
  slow fat production.
- Chitosan (or chitin, the substance found in the exoskeleton of shrimp and
  other shellfish) claims to block fat from being absorbed.

product "boosts the immune system" without first having
to meet any burden of evidence. The FDA has no power
to regulate such a claim.

Supplement manufacturers quickly found ways to
use DSHEA to make health claims under the structure-
or-function clause, without actually making any *specific*
claims. In effect, DSHEA gave these companies free
reign to commit fraud so long as they were careful about
the wording!

In addition, DSHEA declared that herbal remedies
would be regulated as dietary supplements as long as they
were not marketed with the type of claims that are re-
served for pharmaceuticals; in other words, disease-spe-
cific claims. For instance, a company cannot legally claim
that a supplement *cures* cancer. It can, however, claim
that its product *enhances* the immune system's ability to
fight cancer. As long as companies restrict themselves

Natural but Dangerous

One of the most popular natural weight-loss supplements in the 1990s was a powerful amphetamine-like stimulant called ephedra (the Chinese herb *ma huang*), which, in combination with caffeine, triggered measurable weight loss. Unfortunately, because it sped the heart rate, ephedra also dramatically increased the risk of heart attack and stroke. Ephedra is related to epinephrine (adrenaline), which, during times of stress, constricts blood vessels, elevates heart rate, and gets the body ready to fight or flee. At least 155 people died from taking medications containing ephedra. In late 2003, the FDA announced that it would ban the sale of all ephedra-containing drugs. In response, manufacturers began removing the ingredient from their products and now produce ephedra-free versions.

to structure-or-function claims, their product is legally a supplement, and it is therefore free of FDA regulations. This means, in effect, that companies can decide for themselves whether or not their products are classified legally as nutritional supplements simply by restricting themselves to certain kinds of claims and avoiding certain others.

These companies deliver their products to consumers by means of several loopholes in the law. This may seem like splitting hairs, but the law is a precise instrument. Most of the time that precision protects us; sometimes, unfortunately, it can be abused, in which case it becomes a scalpel so precise that it can indeed split hairs!

The FDA does handle post-marketing safety for these products. This means simply that *after* complaints or reports arise that harm has already occurred (such as happened with the dietary supplement ephedra), *then* the FDA can step in and investigate.

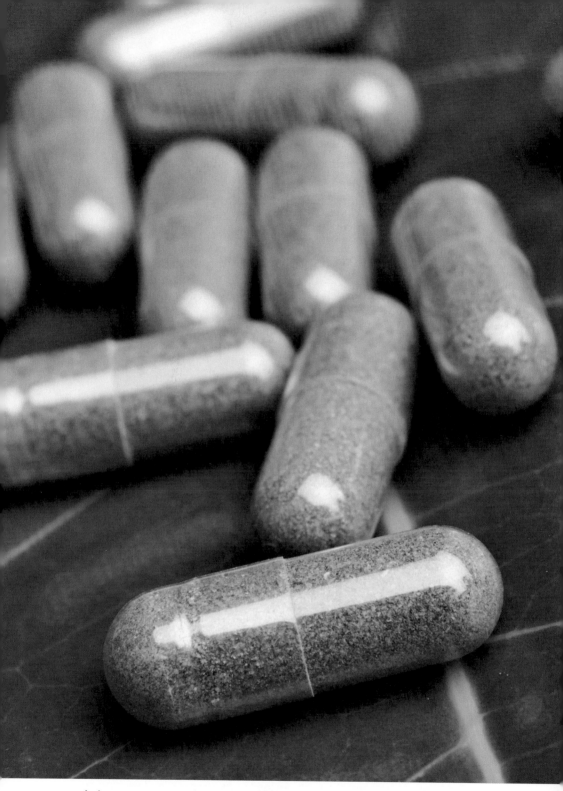

As long as companies do not claim their herbal supplements cure a disease, then they fall outside the regulations of the FDA.

Natural and Everyday Drugs: A False Sense of Security

Right now, although herbal extracts are used in the same way as drugs, they are marketed as supplements. Therefore, the FDA does not have to test the extracts before they appear on the market.

The Law vs. Science

When DSHEA was passed, it created a new definition of nutritional supplement, a legal definition as opposed to the scientific definition. The more scientifically accurate definition for a nutritional supplement would be "a substance taken for its nutritional value, such as vitamins and minerals." From a scientific perspective, a substance is a nutrient if it provides calories, essential proteins, fatty acids, vitamins, or minerals. A nutritional supplement would then by definition provide a nutrient or nutrients to supplement what we get from food.

A drug, however, is not a nutrient. Instead, drugs exert pharmacological effects on the body; they alter the biochemical function of the body, usually by binding to receptors on or inside cells to alter the balance of biochemical reactions and produce a physiological effect. Drugs may also be targeted against microbes invading the body.

So are substances derived from plants and other sources found in nature nutritional supplements or drugs? Typically, these substances contain dozens or hundreds of chemical substances, most of which have little or no nutritional value. These substances are primarily used for their pharmacological effects. In other words, they are drugs. DSHEA, however, allows them to be marketed as supplements, not based upon how they are used or the kinds of effects they have in the body but solely on the type of claims that are made for them by their manufacturers.

Meanwhile, the Federal Trade Commission regulates supplements' truth-in-advertising the same way it would any product. If companies commit actual fraud in their marketing (which is hard to do given the leeway they are provided), then they can be fined. The fines usually amount to a slap on the wrist compared to the millions of dollars most supplements earn their companies. As a result, many of these manufacturers simply regard the risk of fines as an acceptable cost of doing business. And

The secret ingredient in many dietary supplements is caffeine. Caffeine is an alkaloid chemical that acts as a stimulant.

North Americans continue to consume chemicals in the form of dietary supplements.

But dietary supplements are not the only source of chemicals that can affect our bodies without our full awareness. One of the most ordinary and everyday chemicals is caffeine. Many dietary supplements' so-called secret ingredient is actually caffeine—but we're far more apt to encounter caffeine at breakfast or some other mealtime. After all, it's become a standard part of daily life in North America.

Who Discovered Coffee?

According to legend, priests observed that their goats seemed livelier after they munched on a particular berry that grew wild on the mountainside. Curious, the priests made the first caffeinated drink out of coffee-bean husks. They then used the liquid to keep them awake for all-night prayer sessions.

What Is the Federal Trade Commission?

The Federal Trade Commission (FTC) is not a health agency; its professionals are primarily lawyers, economists, and marketing specialists who are not trained to determine the safety and health effects of substances. Therefore, if the FTC allows a claim to be made in advertising, that does not mean that the product actually works; it may just mean that the FTC did not think it was an unfair marketing practice. This is very different from how over-the-counter drugs such as aspirin and antacids are regulated by the FDA. In those cases, the FDA makes sure that the drugs work and works with the manufacturers to develop accurate labeling—and then the FTC is charged with seeing that marketing is consistent with the FDA approval.

What's the bottom line? Well, for ordinary consumers there is no easy way to find out if a dietary supplement actually works or meets the promises made by its advertising!

North America's Favorite Chemical

Chemically speaking, caffeine is an alkaloid, a kind of **compound** that occurs naturally in many plants, including coffee beans, tea leaves, cola beans, cacao beans (the important ingredient in chocolate), and **mate**, as well as other plants. These compounds vary somewhat from plant to plant; they have somewhat different **biochemical** effects, and they are present in different ratios in the different plant sources. What they all have in common is that they stimulate the central nervous system, cardiac muscle, and the respiratory system. They also have a diuretic effect (they make your body eliminate fluids more quickly from its cells), and they delay fatigue.

Today, caffeine can be found in everything from your morning cup of coffee to the Coke you drink at lunchtime to the chocolate bar you have for an after-school snack. In fact, most carbonated soft drinks sold in North America

The compound we know best as caffeine occurs naturally in many plants, includ-ing tea leaves. In each plant, the compound is present in varying amounts and has slightly different biochemical effects.

Coffee Facts and Figures

- A study of java-drinking trends by the National Coffee Association showed that, as of 2011, over half (54%) of all adults aged 24-39 drink coffee every day.
- The coffee industry rakes in an estimated $40 billion per year.
- As a nation, the United States downs 350 million cups of coffee a day.
- The number of teens drinking coffee in restaurants or cafes increased 12 percent in 2006.
- Caffeine has no nutritional value, is not needed for any physiologic function, and is commonly abused by the tired and stressed.
- Coffee can sometimes trigger gastrointestinal distress.

contain caffeine. It's also found in over-the-counter *analgesics*, many cold remedies, weight-loss pills, and many of the dietary supplements we've already discussed. And as Starbucks takes the continent by storm, making coffee drinks like lattes and cappuccinos increasingly popular, North America's love affair with coffee grows ever more passionate!

Drinking coffee and other caffeine-containing beverages is just a fact of North American life. It used to be these were considered grown-up drinks that could "stunt your growth"—but nowadays, more and more teenagers are imbibing caffeine, whether in their soda or their coffee. And let's not forget chocolate! A candy bar can also contain a hefty dollop of caffeine. But what is caffeine, really?

Caffeine's molecular structure is very similar to that of adenosine, an inhibitory brain substance found in many animals, including humans. Animal studies show that adenosine can induce sleep, so it may seem odd that

Caffeine is also found in the pods of the cacao tree. These oval pods are the source of the most important ingredient in chocolate.

How Much Caffeine Is in Your Soda?

According to the National Soft Drink Association, the following is the caffeine content (in mgs) per 12-ounce can of soda:

Jolt	71.2
Sugar-Free Mr. Pibb	58.8
Mountain Dew	55.0 (no caffeine in Canada)
Diet Mountain Dew	55.0
Kick citrus	54.0
Mello Yellow	52.8
Surge	51.0
Tab	46.8
Battery energy drink	46.7
Coca-Cola	45.6
Diet Coke	45.6
Shasta Cola	44.4
Shasta Cherry Cola	44.4
Shasta Diet Cola	44.4
Mr. Pibb	40.8
Dr. Pepper	39.6
Pepsi Cola	37.2
Diet Pepsi	35.4
RC Cola	36.0
Diet RC	36.0
Canada Dry Cola	30.0
Canada Dry Diet Cola	1.2
7 Up	0

caffeine's structure would be similar to this chemical's. Here's how it works.

When people need sleep, their adenosine levels are high, which seems to trigger the brain into wanting to shut down. The longer you're awake, the more adenosine gradually accumulates in your brain. This surplus binds

Since chocolate is derived from the pods of the cacao tree, candy bars also have caffeine in them. Even if you do not drink coffee, you can ingest a lot of caffeine every day.

How Much Caffeine Is in Your Cup?

The variations in the amount of caffeine in a cup of coffee or tea are relatively large, even if the same person using the same equipment and ingredients day after day prepares it. The following numbers are average milligrams of caffeine per average serving for that particular form of beverage.

drip	115–175
espresso	100
brewed	80–135
instant	65–100
decaf, brewed	3–4
decaf, instant	2–3
tea, iced	70
tea, brewed, imported	60
tea, brewed, U.S.	40
tea, instant	30
mate	25–150
hot chocolate	3–8

Caffeine in Chocolate?

A quarter of a cup of chocolate chips has 13–15 milligrams of caffeine. A typical chocolate candy bar has about 30 milligrams.

to specialized adenosine receptors, depressing nervous-system activity and making you groggy. Getting sufficient sleep clears the chemical from your system. But there's an alternative to clearing adenosine from your body by going to sleep: instead, you can block it before it has a chance to make you sleepy. Caffeine does this by binding to adenosine receptors before the adenosine gets there. This is why a cup of coffee or a can of Pepsi can help you stay awake when you're studying late at night.

2 If Something's Natural, How Can It Be Dangerous?

Somehow, North American culture has gotten the idea that medical science can't be trusted. Human viewpoints sometimes are like the swing of a pendulum: as the twentieth century reached its mid-point, most North Americans believed science had the answers to all human ills, from tonsillitis to pneumonia, measles to high-risk pregnancies—but by the beginning of the twenty-first century, the pendulum had swung the other direction, and people had become cynical about modern medicine. AIDS had come along, a disease so frightening and mysterious that science seemed to have no answers. What's more, medical science had made some terrible mistakes, and some of the miracle drugs that promised to offer so much instead had dangerous and unpredicted side effects. Our industrial world that at first seemed designed to make all our lives easier has instead introduced dangerous toxins into the environment, endangering both the planet and human life. Many people feel disappointed

Care and Commonsense

Obviously, science can be a powerful tool—and powerful tools can be dangerous. That doesn't mean they're not useful. A power saw can be used to create houses and save human labor; it can also cut your hand off or even kill you if you're not careful. The medicines offered to us by the scientific world should be used with care and common sense, the same way you would use any other powerful tool.

and disillusioned. Some have begun looking elsewhere for medical answers.

Alternative forms of medicine have become popular. A simpler, more natural approach to medicine sometimes seems safer than one based on the complicated world of scientific research. According to this perspective, if we all went back to the wisdom of our ancestors, doctoring ourselves with berries and bark, we'd be healthier.

Alternative medicine can offer valuable insights; and certainly, we can learn from the past. But we should not forget that in many cases, today's medicine is actually built on yesterday's. Our great-grandparents may have used willow bark to treat a headache; today, pharmaceutical companies deliver the same chemical to us in the form of aspirin. And modern-day pharmaceutical companies are also learning from native people around the world about new plants with healing properties; by studying the chemical properties of these plants, scientists develop new drugs that can help heal bodies and save lives.

After all, science is built on the natural world. Chemicals are not necessarily artificial substances, created by scientists in laboratories. Instead, they are the building blocks of life. Nature itself is made up of chemicals.

Dietary supplements often contain these chemicals that occur naturally in the environment. Some of these

Some people do not trust medical science. These people may turn to alternative forms of medicine instead.

Natural and Everyday Drugs: A False Sense of Security 31

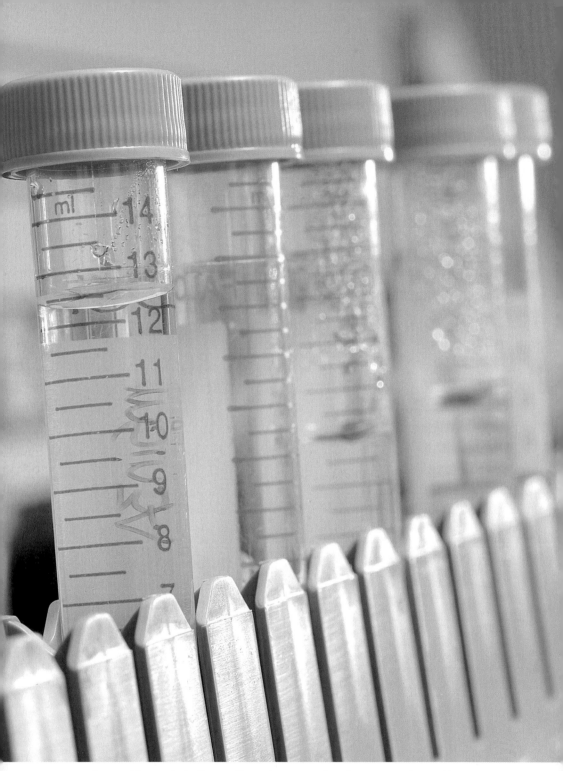

One problem with the "natural" supplements is that they are not thoroughly tested before being released to the public. Companies may see a result in a test tube that does not actually transfer safely to use by people.

Another Dangerous Diet Pill

In the mid-'90s, after DSHEA was passed, the diet pill industry skyrocketed. By 1996, more than 18 million dieters in the United States were taking a prescription cocktail of "natural" appetite suppressants fenfluramine (or dexfenfluramine) and phentermine, nicknamed fen-phen, many with great success. But suddenly, doctors around the country were seeing previously healthy patients who were taking fen-phen developing a potentially fatal heart disease. In September 1997, the FDA announced that it was withdrawing the "fen" drugs from the market because of their link to heart problems. Phentermine is still available on its own as a prescription medicine.

have very little, if any, effect on the human body. Others, however, do have the ability to influence mood, metabolism, or other body functions. These natural remedies are not necessarily bad. Without a doubt, some are effective health aids. So what's the problem?

Inadequate Research

One problem with these "supplements" is that they are not thoroughly tested. This means that if you take an untested supplement, you are serving as the manufacturer's unpaid guinea pig —and you may be risking your own health.

The manufacturers don't wish to pay the huge amounts of money required to conduct the research and testing required to pass the FDA's rigorous testing procedures. Although this keeps prices down for consumers, it also allows manufacturers to get rich quick. The manufacturers market their products as non-drugs, which largely frees them of the burden of having to provide information to the public about the real effectiveness—or dangers—of their products.

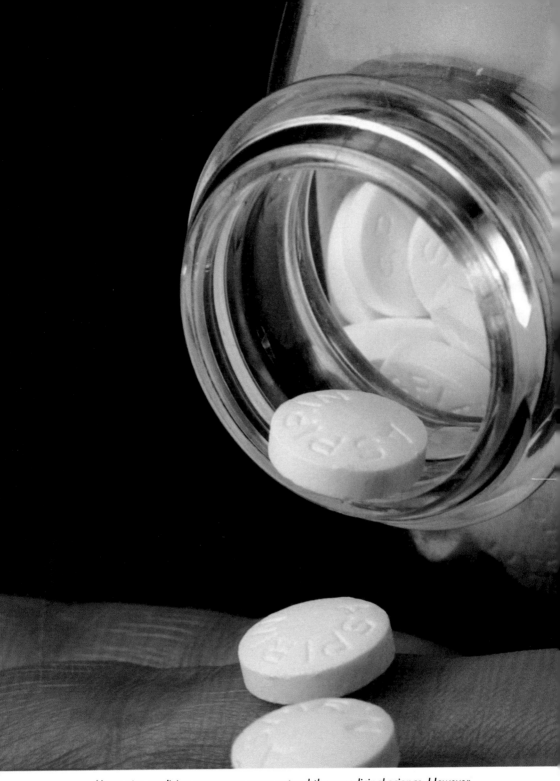

Alternative medicine may seem more natural than medicinal science. However, many medicines, such as aspirin, are derived from natural substances found in plants.

Do "Fat Magnets" Work?

Some of the natural diet products still on the market advertise themselves as "fat magnets." The principal ingredient of these products is chitosan, crushed-up shellfish shells. Manufacturers claim that chitosan has a positive ionic charge, which attracts negatively charged fat like a magnet, reducing the absorption of fat from the gut and thus reducing the absorption of cholesterol.

Is this true? Scientists really can't say, because not enough research has been done to either prove or disprove the claim. Doctors, however, point out that a potential problem with chitosan is that it may block the absorption of fat-soluble vitamins such as vitamins A, D, and K, which means long-term use may lead to a deficiency of these vitamins.

Sometimes companies that produce dietary supplements claim their products' benefits are in fact backed by scientific research. Often, however, they are basing *clinical* claims on pre-clinical or basic science studies (by looking at cells and chemicals in test tubes and Petri dishes rather than conducting studies with actual human beings). They may cite a study, for example, that shows that their product increases the activity of T-cells (a type of cell in the immune system) *in vitro*. They then use this data to support the claim that their product "enhances the immune system"—or even cures cancer—but meanwhile, the precise relationships are not clear between in-vitro observations and the ultimate clinical implications in human beings. In this case, increasing the activity of certain T-cells may have no benefit to the functioning of the immune system—or it may even be harmful by causing autoimmune destructive effects. Researchers know that for every substance eventually found to be safe and effective in people, there are hundreds of substances that initially looked promising in the test tube.

According to *Fat-Exploding the Myths* by Lisa Colles, Americans spend between $30 and $50 billion each year on diet and weight-loss programs, products, and pills; $6 billion of this is said to be spent on so-called natural weight-loss products and pills that are fraudulent.

Deceptive Marketing

Companies that manufacture these natural drugs typically use a combination of marketing strategies, each of which may be legal—but together they work to deceive the consumer. For example, companies will often ask physicians or other health professionals to endorse their products. These "hired guns" are careful not to make any specific health claims; often all they say is that the product is "healthy" and that they recommend its use. Another component of many natural drug marketing strategies is to make precisely those claims that are allowed by DSHEA: that the products boost the immune system, detoxify the body, enhance energy, improve mental function, and other structure-and-function claims. Yet another marketing component is the use of **testimonials**. This allows companies to relate what others are claiming about their products, while not making the claim themselves.

Do You Know What You're Taking?

One of the big problems with natural supplements is that consumers can't be sure what they're actually consuming. If you take a drug that's been approved by the FDA—say Tylenol® for a headache, for example, or an antibiotic for

Natural—But Not Necessarily Safe

Aloe

Long used to treat burns and wounds, aloe, when ingested, also causes a strong and urgent need to defecate. Because of that effect, aloe is often marketed as an internal cleanser. Supplements that cause reactions like this are not likely to be safe to take internally, as diarrhea is a warning sign of some potentially dangerous conditions. Although aloe is soothing and can promote healing when applied to the skin, no proof has been offered that ingested aloe helps promote weight loss.

Dandelion

Dandelion—yes, those fuzzy yellow flowers that dot the lawn—has also recently entered the market as a weight-loss supplement. A natural diuretic, dandelion causes frequent urination and can reduce the water weight a person carries. Many people are allergic to this supplement, and it can cause severe dehydration in long-term users. Some research has shown that dandelion may be carcinogenic, causing cancers in laboratory rats.

Guarana

In Brazil, native people have long known that the seeds of a certain plant have a stimulating effect when eaten or ground up and mixed with water or tea. Today, guarana is common in herbal remedy sections, as it speeds up metabolism and promotes frequent urination. One of the components of guarana extract is caffeine. Guarana often interacts with medicines and can cause deadly complications in certain cases. The extract has some relatively powerful anticlotting properties and can cause unstoppable bleeding in long-term users.

Guar Gum

The Indian cluster bean is the source of yet another powerful herbal extract. Guar gum is a type of dietary fiber, often used as a thickening substance in cooking or in medications. The action of guar gum is like a sponge; it absorbs water rapidly and swells up to twenty times its original size in the process. Some people who have used this substance to curb their appetites have had very dangerous intestinal blockages, requiring surgery to remove. Guar gum also causes rapid blood sugar changes, so diabetics must take extreme care in taking it.

a nasal infection—you can be certain that each tablet or capsule holds exactly the same amount of the drug as all the others—and that when you buy a new bottle of the medicine, each one of those tablets will be exactly as powerful as the first batch. What's more, if you buy a generic brand of acetaminophen (the drug that's in Tylenol), you can be certain that it will be just as strong as the same dosage of Tylenol. But that's not the case with natural drugs. If you buy a dietary supplement such as St. John's wort, which helps balance moods, or goldthread to help you fight off a virus, you can never be sure exactly how much of the effective agent you're getting. One company's may be stronger and more effective than an-

Companies that manufacture natural drugs hire health professionals to endorse their products. The doctors make no specific health claims, but they deceive viewers into thinking that the product is "healthy."

Dandelions have recently entered stores as a weight-loss supplement. However, the bright yellow flowers can be very dangerous, causing severe dehydration and possibly cancer.

"Natural" Highs?

Some people turn to natural substances to alter their consciousness—in other words, get high. Marijuana is probably the best known of these natural highs, but there are plenty of other plants that have psychoactive effects. Many of these can also be toxic—especially if you're not exactly sure what to look for. Here are some examples.

- Certain kinds of mushrooms cause psychedelic effects similar to LSD. Many mushrooms, however, are also deadly.
- Morning glory seeds can act as a hallucinogen, also similar to LSD. They also cause nausea.
- Nutmeg can create euphoria when ingested in large enough quantities. It can also cause nausea, impaired motor functions, and speech impairments. "Nutmeg highs" are usually followed by long, coma-like periods of sleep of sixteen hours or more.
- Betel nuts cause a mild "high" similar to nicotine or caffeine. Habitual chewing of these nuts also can cause mouth cancer.

other's; the same company's supplements may even vary from batch to batch.

You also may not know exactly what's in many natural drugs. Because it's not always clear what goes into some supplements, people with food allergies should be particularly wary. Some supplements contain ingredients from shellfish and other potential allergens.

When it comes to supplements, be a skeptical consumer. Do as much research as you can on a particular product, using reputable Web sites. Ask your doctor's advice. Most of us like the sound of getting "back to nature." But if something sounds too good to be true—sometimes it is!

3 So What's Wrong with Caffeine?

Molly knows better than to bug her mom in the morning. Until her mother's had her first cup of coffee, there's no point talking to her. All she'll do is grunt, while she staggers around the kitchen, her face haggard with weariness. Just let her get some coffee inside her, though, and by the time the two of them are out the door on the way to school, her mother is chatting and smiling.

Derek knows he probably shouldn't leave his homework until late at night. But between basketball practice and his job, by the time he has a chance to sit down with his books, it always seems to be at least eleven o'clock. He's learned, though, that if he sips a tall glass of Coke while he studies, he can usually stay alert enough to do a good job.

Liz loves lattes. Some mornings, especially when it's cold outside, the only thing that motivates her to get out of bed and get dressed for school

What's an Addiction?

We use the word addiction a lot in today's world. It's used for medical conditions like alcoholism and substance abuse. It's also used for destructive behaviors like gambling, unhealthy sex, and even shopping. And people also use it in reference to ordinary substances—like sugar and yes, caffeine.

From a medical perspective, however, addiction is a chronic relapsing condition, characterized by compulsive drug seeking and abuse, and by long-lasting chemical changes in the brain. An addictive substance induces pleasant states or relieves distress—but continued use of the addictive substance induces adaptive changes in the brain that lead to tolerance, physical dependence, uncontrollable craving and, all too often, relapse. Stopping the drug becomes very difficult and causes severe physical and mental reactions.

is the thought of the latte she'll buy at the coffee shop across the street from the high school. The cup will be warm in her cold hands, the rich creamy beverage will comfort her, and by the time she tosses the cup in the trash in her homeroom, she will be ready for her day.

Can Coffee Kill You?

Yes—if you drank somewhere between fifty and two hundred cups in one sitting. However, a single package of NoDoz® could as well!

North Americans love caffeine. We sip it when we get together with friends. We use it to rev up in the morning—and we use it as a pick-me-up when we're dragging. (Why else would coffee breaks be such an established part of many

Caffeine is a normal part of many people's lives. Friends often get together at cafés to enjoy some coffee and conversation.

Natural and Everyday Drugs: A False Sense of Security 45

How Dangerous Is Caffeine?

• Caffeine has been linked to possible dangers to unborn children. Pregnant rats that received daily dosages of caffeine comparable to seventy cups a day for a human did give birth to malformed offspring. Although no pregnant woman is likely to be drinking seventy cups of coffee a day, moderation during pregnancy seems to be the wisest course when it comes to coffee, tea, cola, and other caffeinated drinks.

• Caffeine can reduce the motility of men's sperm, thus making it more difficult for conception to occur.

• Drinking caffeinated beverages has been associated with increased incidents of decreased bone density in the hips and spine, particularly among women. Drinking at least a glass of milk a day, however, counteracts this effect.

workdays?) We depend on it to keep us awake when we pull all-nighters during exam week or when we want to be sure we're alert enough to drive. So is there a problem with that?

Some people think there is—but others disagree. Caffeine certainly isn't a dangerous drug like amphetamines or cocaine; it doesn't act on the areas of the brain related to reward, motivation, and addiction. You might find yourself craving your daily caffeine fix—but that doesn't mean you're addicted.

But it *is* possible to overdose on caffeine. Too much caffeine can even produce a psychiatric disorder called caffeine-induced organic mental disorder. According to the most recent version of the American Psychiatric Association's *Diagnostic and Statistical Manual of Mental*

Some coffee drinkers may not think it is true, but it is possible to drink too much coffee. It can lead to an overdose of caffeine, which is known as "caffeine intoxication."

Natural and Everyday Drugs: A False Sense of Security 47

The American Psychiatric Association also includes caffeine withdrawal in the DSM. Withdrawal explains the headaches and lethargy regular caffeine users may experience if they go without their coffee or soft drinks for a day or so. For example, a person who drinks coffee throughout the day at work, may feel lazy and headachey on the weekend when she doesn't drink as much coffee—or teens drinking lots of soft drinks all summer often feel slow and fuzzy the first week of school when suddenly they're not drinking the same amounts of soft drinks.

Disorders, the DSM-IV-TR, this disorder is caused by "caffeine intoxication." It must meet the following criteria:

1. Recent consumption of caffeine, usually in excess of 250 mg.

2. At least five of the following signs:
   - restlessness
   - nervousness
   - excitement
   - insomnia
   - flushed face
   - diuresis
   - gastrointestinal disturbance
   - muscle twitching
   - rambling flow of thought and speech
   - *tachycardia* or *cardiac arrhythmia*
   - periods of inexhaustibility
   - *psychomotor* agitation

3. Not due to any physical or other mental disorder, such as an anxiety disorder.

Many people enjoy a cup of coffee as a part of their morning ritual. One cup of coffee cannot lead to caffeine intoxication.

Natural and Everyday Drugs: A False Sense of Security 49

Another side effect of caffeine intoxication is the need to run to the bathroom repeatedly. Caffeine is a diuretic, which causes frequent urination, but it may also cause gastrointestinal problems.

50 Chapter 3—So What's Wrong With Caffeine?

Basically, overdosing on caffeine is not a very pleasant experience—but it's not likely that you'll die from it or even have any permanent damage. Despite that, as experts note that teenagers are becoming more and more fond of caffeinated beverages, many North Americans are becoming concerned.

 Teens and Caffeine

For the past few years, eighteen-year-old Pam Shelton told a reporter from ABC News, she's been drinking about ten caffeinated drinks a day. "I probably have three cups of coffee and the rest soda," she says. Meanwhile, Terry Kleeblatt, also eighteen, figures he averages about eight a day. "I drink a lot of Diet Coke all day [and] coffee, lot of ice coffee, every day," he says. At 50 to 100 milligrams of caffeine per drink, both probably consume at least 500 milligrams of caffeine a day. "The safe recommended intake for caffeine for adults is between 200 and 300 milligrams a day," Rachel Brandeis from the American Dietetic Association, told ABC News in 2004.

It's a concern that's getting more and more media attention. In a December 2002 article in the *Chronicle Deputy*, for example, Sam McManis reported that teens have a "new drug of choice":

Teenage caffeine consumption, once limited to sodas and hot chocolate, now has nearly become the norm in the Bay Area and nationally. Though no statistics exist to chart teenage coffee drinkers—the National Coffee Association polls only consumers 18 and older—a drive past any coffeehouse near a high school would show that it's replaced the iconic malt shop of the '50s or 7-Eleven of the '70s as the place to socialize. . . .

Coffee shops today are a popular place for teens to gather and socialize. They seem to be the modern equivalent of the malt shop in the '50s.

Most teens don't consider themselves java junkies. But the amount of caffeine they consume in a few Frappuccinos or espressos with friends adds up. And the caffeine in sodas and "energy drinks" adds to their caffeine intake. Some teens also use caffeine pills, such as Vivarin® or NoDoz®, to study late at night or stay alert in morning classes. . . .

Andre O'Brien and Renalen Chanco, both 16 and juniors at Berkeley High, stopped by the Starbucks on Shattuck Avenue after school one recent afternoon for iced lattes. The two are regulars, but they say they aren't addicted to caffeine. They can stop whenever they like, honest.

"I started at 14; it was a social thing," Andre said. "When you go to Starbucks, what else are you going to do except drink when you talk? But I

The National Coffee Association only polls consumers 18 and older. However, many teens are becoming coffee drinkers at much younger ages.

Natural and Everyday Drugs: A False Sense of Security

Many students are very busy with activities outside of school. Therefore, they drink a lot of coffee and soda to stay awake and focused during class.

Students are expected to complete a lot of homework each night. Caffeinated beverages allow students to stay awake later in order to finish all their assignments.

don't like straight coffee. It's too strong. My dad's the one addicted. He can't even go a morning without it."

Chanco laughed when asked whether she feels dependent on caffeine.

"Does coffee ice cream count?" she asked. "Because I've been eating that since I was 4 years old. I have a lot of mocha Frappuccinos. It gives a good kick. In addition to coffee, there's chocolate in it. That has caffeine, right? Chocolate's good. Very good."

Simon Ortiz acknowledges her addiction to the coffee bean. As a correspondent for Youth Radio, she even broadcast an essay about her addiction on KQED. She wrote: "When I started drinking

Coffee can easily become a part of a student's normal breakfast routine. However, getting into the habit of drinking coffee every day can make the days without coffee very difficult.

coffee, I didn't think I'd become addicted. I figured . . . I could quit anytime. Turns out, I was incredibly wrong. A few times, I forgot to drink coffee in the morning. By the afternoon, I had this huge headache. I was drowsy, and my temper was through the roof. It took about two years of this dependency to realize myself that caffeine wasn't good for my body."

But Simon Ortiz still has been unable to kick the caffeine habit.

"I'm still trying to come to terms with it," she said, laughing. "I've tried to stop several times, but it really hasn't worked. I tried to go down to half decaf, half caf, but . . . I've gotten less and less OK with drinking coffee. It bothers me that I'm more addicted to it than when I started. I don't like the

Developing a bad headache after skipping your morning cup of coffee is a sign that you have a dependency on coffee. You may also feel drowsy and have a short temper.

Natural and Everyday Drugs: A False Sense of Security 59

Specialty coffee shops are common in most towns. Students frequent them to socialize and get a boost of energy from a cappuccino or latte.

One of the sources of caffeine most commonly ingested by teens is energy drinks. They pack in a lot of caffeine, usually more than coffee and tea. Some of the most common energy drinks can have up to 300 mg of caffeine.

headaches and tiredness when I don't drink it, but I don't necessarily like the way I feel when I do drink it."

Some teenage caffeine drinkers proudly acknowledge their vice. Joanna DeLeon, 18, started drinking Frappuccinos in middle school in Union City. She got hooked. Now a freshman at UC Santa Cruz, DeLeon says java junkies abound on campus. She calls it the only legal high left.

"I did it at first to stay awake," she said. "Soda doesn't do it for me. Now I'll drink a Frappuccino, and it's kind of bitter. Five minutes later, I'll be babbling. I had espresso for the first time the other day. That was crazy. I drank it at 10 (p.m.) and didn't get to sleep until 5 a.m. And I wanted to go to sleep. I'm, like, 'Whoa, this is not good.'"

Clearly, this newspaperman thinks teens and coffee aren't a good mix. In fact, he makes it sound as though coffee may be the next dangerous drug habit that kids are going to have to battle. And he's not the only one who's thinking along these lines. In 2004, Sylvia Perez of ABC News had this to say about teens and coffee:

There's a new love affair brewing between children and coffee and it's a relationship that gives some health professionals the jitters.

Natural and Everyday Drugs: A False Sense of Security 61

A cup of coffee does not look threatening. However, some people view coffee as the next dangerous drug habit that teens will have to battle.

Should High Schools' Days Begin Later?

A few studies have been conducted investigating the effects of a later start to the school day. Researchers have surveyed students, teachers, parents, administrators, coaches, area employers of students, and others. The studies show that when school opens later, more students graduate, remain continuously enrolled, attend school more days, and more often show up on time. Alcohol and other drug dependence also decreased, as did the use of tobacco and caffeine.

Specialty coffee shops are everywhere these days and an increasingly popular place for kids to hang out. With long school hours and days packed with extra curricular activities, teens are finding a cup of coffee can provide a quick burst of energy. . . .

Lattes, mochas, coolattas, and other caffeine-laced beverages are increasingly becoming the drink of choice for high school teenagers. . . .

We caught up with several fourteen year olds at a coffee shop across from their school in Chicago's Lincoln Park area.

"Probably like 90-percent of my friends drink coffee or coffee flavored and tea and stuff like that," said Yassar Bittar.

The younger generation has taken to the drinks that taste more like a milkshake than a simple cup of joe.

"It has a caramel coffee taste in it and it's iced," said one teen.

And across the country teens say it's as much about being social as getting a caffeine fix.

"Right after school on a normal day it is pretty packed," said Michael Levay.

An important part of being a teenager is socializing and hanging out with friends. If her friends are all going to the local coffee shop, a teen is likely to go as well.

What is wrong with teens drinking coffee? One concern is that the powerful stimulant effects of caffeine may be too much for growing bodies.

But what many teens may not know is that caffeine is a powerful **stimulant**, and for young, growing bodies it can be too much.

"I don't think people realize that caffeine is really a drug and it's very addictive," said Cynthia Mears, D.O. She is a teen medicine specialist with Children's Memorial Hospital. . . . "It causes your heart rate to go up, it causes you to have increased diuresis which means you urinate more frequently and when you go through caffeine withdrawal you get depressed and irritated," Dr. Mears said.

So are articles like these exaggerating in order to create an interesting news story? Or are they drawing attention to a legitimate concern? As a teenager, should you worry about how much coffee you drink?

Legitimate Concerns

No, coffee probably isn't going to ruin your life. It's not going to turn you into a desperate drug addict. There probably won't ever be a Caffeine Anonymous group,

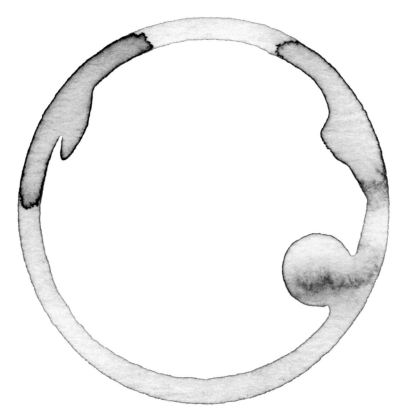

Drinking too much coffee during the day can cause insomnia at night, which will lead to extreme drowsiness the next day. More coffee will be drunk to get through the drowsiness and a vicious coffee circle will be the result.

Drinking coffee may not be as dangerous as smoking, or drinking alcohol. However, withdrawal from coffee can cause depression and irritability.

Natural and Everyday Drugs: A False Sense of Security 67

Like any chemical, caffeine has an effect on the body and its functions. One of the biggest concerns for teenagers and coffee is how it affects their sleep patterns.

Coffee Shops and Teens

North Americans are in love with coffee drinks, and coffee shops have become one of their favorite hangouts. Starbucks is one of the fastest growing of these chains—and teenagers have done their share in making Starbucks popular. Nutrition experts have criticized coffee chains like Starbucks for using sweetened coffee drinks as so-called starter beverages that get young people hooked on caffeine. Starbucks' written policy, however, says its "overall marketing, advertising and event sponsorship efforts are not directed at children or youth," although some "community activities" end up reaching kids. The company reviews marketing materials to avoid distributing ones that could be "inadvertently appealing to youth," the policy says. "Starbucks itself is a gathering place," says Brad Stevens, Starbucks vice president of U.S. marketing. "You can often go in and see a whole family." Some coffee chains say nutritional and other concerns shouldn't stop them from trying to attract young customers. "Better they should get hooked on an ice-blended beverage than maybe something else," says Michael Coles, president and chief executive of Caribou Coffee Co., a Minneapolis-based coffee chain with 410 stores. Parents have thanked him for giving their kids a place to do homework, he says.

where members stand up and say, "Hi, my name is Bob (or Jane), and I'm addicted to cappuccinos."

However, that doesn't mean you shouldn't be aware of the effects coffee and other caffeinated beverages can have on your body. Caffeine is a chemical—and like many other chemicals, it has the power to change the way your body operates. Two of the most legitimate concerns about teens and caffeine have to do with how it affects adolescent sleep patterns and adolescent nutritional habits.

Teens and Sleep Patterns

If you're a teenager, you probably already know that you never seem to have enough sleep. When you were

How Many Calories in Your Frap?

A sixteen-ounce grande-size Strawberries & Crème Frappuccino made with whole milk and whipped cream has 370 calories and 15 grams of fat. By comparison, the same size Frappé Mocha at McDonald's has 560 calories and 24 grams of fat. As of June 2007, however, Starbucks makes all of its Frappuccinos with 2% milk unless whole milk is requested. This lowers the calorie count by 10. Subtract the whipped cream and the calorie count drops by another 120!

younger, your parents probably set your bedtime for you. By eight or nine o'clock, like it or not, you were tucked up for the night—and by seven or eight the next morning, you were wide awake and ready to go. As an adolescent, though, things have changed.

Most teenagers love to stay up late—and they also love to sleep late in the morning. If they had their way, many adolescents would be up talking, using the computer, listening to music, or watching television until well after midnight. And then the following day, they'd sleep through breakfast and maybe even lunch, and then finally be ready to do it all again. These adolescent sleep patterns drive many parents crazy, but research shows that sleep habits like this are more than adolescent rebellion or laziness.

Sometime in late **puberty**, the body starts secreting the sleep-related hormone melatonin at a different time than it did during childhood. This changes the **circadian rhythms** that guide a person's sleep-wake cycle. As a young adult goes through his twenties, the rhythm changes again, but in the meantime, the teen feels wide awake and fully alert at about 7:30 p.m., unlike an adult who is starting to wind down and feel sleepier as the evening progresses so that by 10 or 11 p.m. the adult is ready

Research has shown that teens have a different pattern of hormone secretions than adults. As a result, teens prefer to stay up late at night and sleep in late the next day.

Natural and Everyday Drugs: A False Sense of Security 71

Teenagers usually cannot sleep as much as they want because most school days start early in the morning. Therefore, students turn to coffee to help them stay awake at a time when their bodies want to be asleep.

Parents and teachers reprimand teenagers for staying up late, or falling asleep in class. However, research indicates that these behaviors may have little to do with laziness or lack of self-discipline.

to go to bed. The teenager's wind-down time takes place much later.

Meanwhile, no matter how much young adults would like to stay up late and sleep late the next morning, real life interferes. Most high schools' days begin early, which means teens have to be up as early as 5:30 or 6 a.m. "Just go to bed earlier," parents may chide, but it's really not that simple. Even though a teenager goes to bed at ten, she's likely to lie in bed wide awake until midnight or later, no matter how exhausted she is the next morning.

It's no wonder then that many kids turn to caffeine as a wake-me-up to get them going in the morning. Physicians, however, are concerned that caffeine may only compound a teen's sleep issues, making it more difficult for him to fall asleep at night.

Studies show that most teens are chronically sleep deprived. Coffee may be both a cause of sleep deprivation and a consequence of it.

Dr. Jim Lane, a researcher at Duke University who has studied caffeine's effects on the body, has this to say:

> One aspect of concern for kids is the smaller body size, which means that the same amount of caffeine would have greater, and more long-lasting effects, on them. Research suggests that teens are chronically sleep deprived. Caffeine use might be a consequence of that, and also a cause. Drinking coffee could lead to sleep-onset insomnia, or a delay in going to bed, that contributes to sleep deprivation. I've seen many adolescents develop a morning coffee habit, because school now starts at 7:30 and they had to get up before 6.

Sleep deprivation causes more problems than just sleepiness. Not getting enough sleep can affect memory, and make learning more difficult.

Natural and Everyday Drugs: A False Sense of Security 75

Adolescence is a very stressful time of life. Sleep deprivation can cause fraying emotions to break, leading to more extreme mood swings.

Sleep deprivation also weakens the immune system. A weakened immune system makes a teen more susceptible to illnesses and also makes it harder to recover from them.

So is being sleepy and tired all the time really such a big deal? Many teens seem to take it for granted, just a fact of life that they try to compensate for with marathon sleep sessions on the weekends. But sleep deprivation is a serious issue. It can impair memory and inhibit creativity, making it difficult for sleep-deprived students to learn. Adolescents are already struggling to deal with stress and control their emotions, and sleep deprivation makes the task even more difficult. Irritability, lack of self-confidence and mood swings are often common in teens, but sleep deprivation makes it worse. Depression can result from chronic sleep deprivation. Not enough sleep also endangers the immune system and makes the body more susceptible to illnesses. Judgment can be impaired, which is a particular concern when adolescents are behind the wheel of a car.

Teens and Nutrition

Physicians are also concerned about the ways that caffeinated drinks may be affecting adolescents' nutrition. They're particularly worried about the new frozen coffee drinks that have become so popular. "You're just getting a glass of fat, sugar and caffeine," said one nutritionist.

Researchers have also found that teens who drink a lot of caffeinated drinks are often short on calcium, in part because they usually drink less milk, but also because caffeine depletes calcium that's already in the body. Adolescence is a peak time in terms of growth, especially when it comes to building bone density and bone mass—but increased levels of caffeine can increase calcium excretion through urine.

Caffeinated beverages often contain empty calories. So a teen may feel full after she has a Coke or Pepsi or a cup of coffee with cream and sugar—but caffeine and calories are all she's really given her body for fuel. There are no vitamins or minerals in cola or coffee!

Here are some more facts to consider when deciding how much caffeine you should consume:

- Consuming one twelve-ounce (355-milliliter) sweetened soft drink per day increases a young adult's chance of obesity by 60 percent.
- Drinking too many sweetened caffeinated drinks can lead to dental cavities from the high sugar content and the erosion of the enamel of the teeth from the acidity. One twelve-ounce (355-milliliter) nondiet, carbonated soft drink contains the equivalent of ten teaspoons of sugar (49 milliliters) and 150 calories.

Another downside to drinking too many coffee beverages is the lack of nutri-tional value. In fact, caffeine beverages usually contain a high amount of sugar and fat.

Natural and Everyday Drugs: A False Sense of Security 79

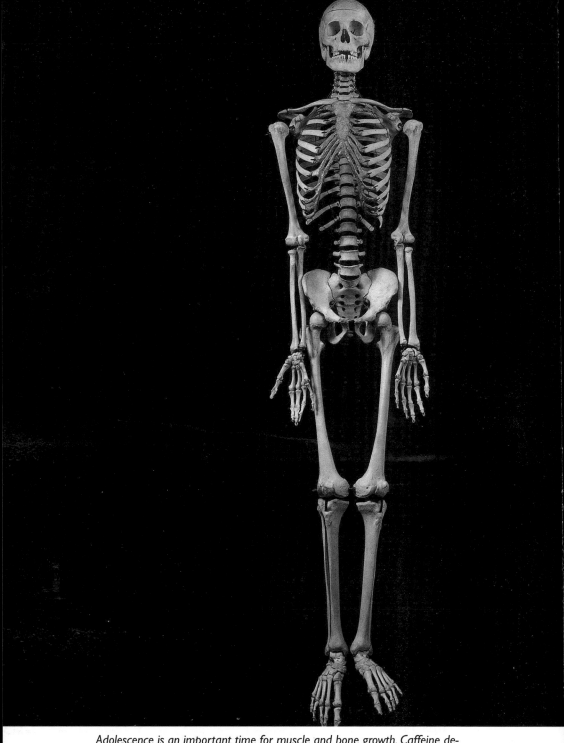

Adolescence is an important time for muscle and bone growth. Caffeine depletes calcium that is necessary for this growth.

Drinking a can of caffeinated soda may give you a boost of energy, but it also delivers a huge serving of sugar. One twelve-ounce can of regular soda is equal to ten teaspoons of sugar.

- Caffeine is a diuretic that causes the body to eliminate water (through urinating), which may contribute to dehydration. Caffeine may be an especially poor choice in hot weather, when you need to replace water lost through perspiration.

But the news isn't all bad. Coffee beverages like lattes offer something a can of soda does not: milk. And milk contains protein, calcium, vitamin D, and vitamin A. Make your latte nonfat, and it's an even healthier alternative.

By being smarter about caffeine intake, teens can drink coffee and still be happy and healthy. Some recommendations include limiting intake to only one coffee beverage a day and recognizing that caffeine may have negative physical effects.

What's Safe?

If you decide to make caffeine a part of your life, physicians recommend that you keep in mind a few things:

- Caffeine causes physical dependence in its users, meaning users go through withdrawal symptoms, which can range from throbbing headaches to fatigue to irritability.
- Caffeine is a chemical that affects mood, behavior and nervous system.
- Teens should consume no more than three caffeinated soda beverages or one super-caffeinated coffee beverage a day.
- If you're hoping to ace a critical exam with a caffeinated boost to your IQ, the current evidence indicates that caffeine doesn't make you smarter!
- Caffeine can have a dramatic effect on alertness but as you move to higher-order cognitive functioning, such as decision-making, it has little impact.
- Too much caffeine has negative physical effects that include, jitteriness and nervousness, upset stomach, headaches, difficulty concentrating, difficulty sleeping, increased heart rate, and increased blood pressure.
- Caffeine can aggravate heart problems or nervous disorders, and some children may not be aware that they're at risk.

But there's one thing that caffeine *doesn't* do: it won't stunt your growth! Although scientists once worried that caffeine could hinder growth, this concern isn't supported by research.

Online Comments from Teens on Caffeine

"In my seventh grade science project . . . I exposed flatworms to caffeine. They *dissolved*."
—sophomore Tony Burnetti

"I know tons of people who stop by Starbucks in the morning to get their 'fix' or else they complain the whole day about how they're tired. I think it has to do with teenagers being worn out from studying, doing sports or participating in another activity. Caffeine gives them a burst of energy they later cannot function without. The school system is to blame for the addiction for overworking the students."
—sophomore Jung Han

"I feel that too many teenagers are addicted to caffeine, because school starts too early and the homework load is humongous. In middle school, I woke up at 7:00 a.m. and left the house around 7:20 a.m. Now, I wake up at 5:45 and leave the house at 6:05 a.m. Waking up early leaves everyone to scrounge around for something to get them through the day. I eat a sweet cereal bar every morning and some of my friends have resorted to caffeine. Coke, Pepsi, coffee (or anything else sold at Starbucks or various bookstores) are what they drink. The caffeine isn't only addictive, it helps them through the day, and it keeps them up. No offense to any teachers, but sitting through an hour and a half of class everyday could easily put anyone to sleep. I drink soda while I do my homework just so that I won't fall asleep while pondering tedious questions. In conclusion, yes, I do think that too many teenagers are addicted to caffeine, but because school (especially high school) starts so early and we have too much homework."
—freshman Ariel La

"I don't consider caffeine an addicting drug. The only times that I remember drinking soda for the purpose of staying awake were a few days last school year near the end of the year. I could force down 3 cans during the night to stay awake, but I'd never crave soda. I stopped drinking soda on a daily basis, for about a month now, and I have had no cravings for caffeine. I don't think teenagers are addicted to caffeine."
—sophomore Pragun Vohra

"[Teenagers are addicted to caffeine because] too many teenagers are expected to be awake before dawn. If you complain about the problem you must attack the cause. Since, as we all know, teenagers are inherently bad, and unconcerned with their own health and well-being, the only solution is to launch a mass propaganda campaign persuading teenagers to wake up at a healthier time, and 'just say no' to caffeine."
—sophomore Brian Lawrence

What do *you* think?

5 Teens and Natural Drugs

It's sometimes called a "mood mix"; other times, it's referred to as "freshmen selection." The Drug Enforcement Agency calls it a "drug of concern"—but it is still legal. Its name is *Salvia divinorum*—and it's all-natural.

In April 2006, ABC news reported the story of one adolescent whose experience with salvia proved to be deadly. Although he ultimately committed suicide, his parents were convinced he would never have taken his life if he hadn't been taking the natural drug.

Salvia is a plant from the mint family. The native people of Mexico have used it for thousands of years for religious purposes. Dr. Ara Dermarderosian, a professor at the University of the Sciences of Philadelphia, has studied salvia for several decades, trying to determine if chemicals in the plant can be used to treat depression and pain. Dr. Dermarderosian reports that ingesting salvia also produces **hallucinogenic** effects that are similar to LSD. "It can be a dream-like state," he told ABC, "it can be a feeling of floating, it can be a feeling of understanding, it can be a feeling of becoming one with nature and so on."

"Once [my son] took that salvia," the deceased boy's mother told ABC, "he wanted to explore and go beyond the boundaries and the

Salvia is a good example of an "all-natural" drug that is very dangerous. Its effects have been compared to the hallucinogenic effects of LSD, which is ingested using blotting paper such as this.

Salvia is a plant from the mint family. Even though at least one teen has died as a result of ingesting salvia, it is still totally legal.

senses that we have here on Earth." She and the boy's father are working to make salvia illegal. In the meantime, however, the FDA does not regulate salvia. Despite its chemical effects on the body, it is not legally considered a drug. "It's not going to bring my son back to have it outlawed," said the mother, "but it may save some lives."

How Dangerous Can an Herb Be?

Researchers disagree on the answer to this question. In most cases, herbal remedies and other dietary supplements are fairly harmless. However, using herbal remedies may indicate more serious problems.

A study conducted at the University of Rochester Medical Center, reported in a 2006 issue of the *Journal*

Can Natural Supplements Give Me a Better Body?

One of the most common reason young adults turn to natural drugs is for help achieving the "perfect body"—one that looks and performs like a movie star's or an athlete's. Herbs like chickweed, ginseng, kelp, and bee pollen are often advertised as diet aids; other herbs, including astragalus, boron, ciwujia, and creatine, are said to enhance athletes' performance. Truth is, though, researchers say these products do little or nothing to deliver the results they promise—and some can be harmful or deadly in large doses.

Ultimately, the only safe and effective way to take off excess pounds and create a strong, well-muscled body is the same as it's always been: healthy eating and exercise.

of Adolescent Health, suggests that adolescents who used herbal supplements are six times more likely to have tried cocaine and almost fifteen times more likely to have used anabolic steroids than teens who have never used herbal products. More than a quarter of the high school students in the sample reported having used herbal remedies and of those, the heaviest herbal users were more likely to use illicit drugs. (Herbal remedies were defined as products that included dietary supplements, such as vitamins or St. John's wort, as well as natural performance enhancers, such as creatine.)

"The study points to the need for parents and health care providers to ask if teens are using herbal remedies and from there probe deeper for possible drug use," study author Susan Yussman told *Consumer Affairs.* Dr. Yussman, assistant professor of pediatrics in the Division of Adolescent Medicine at the university's Golisano Children's Hospital, added, "Children who are open to experimenting with herbal products may be more open to trying illicit drugs."

Studies have shown that teens who use herbal remedies are more likely to try illicit drugs as well. Herbal remedies include dietary supplements, vitamins and St. John's wort.

Natural and Everyday Drugs: A False Sense of Security 91

The search for the "perfect body" leads some teens to try herbal remedies. Athletes trying to enhance performance use astralagus.

The study found that teens who have ever used herbal products (compared to teens who have never used herbal products) are:

- 4.4 times more likely to have ever used inhalants.
- 4.4 times more likely to have ever used LSD, PCP, ecstasy, mushrooms, and other illegal drugs.
- 5.9 times more likely to have ever used cocaine.

Dangerous Herbs

According to a recent report distributed by the Associated Press, a Chinese herb in a weight-loss preparation damaged the kidneys of 105 patients at a Belgian clinic and apparently caused eighteen cases of cancer among them. "Our findings reinforce the idea that the use of natural herbal medicine may not be without risk," Dr. Joelle L. Nortier wrote in the *New England Journal of Medicine*.

Parents should be aware of the apparent connection between the use of herbal remedies and other drug use. Children who are open to experimenting with herbal products may be more open to trying illicit drugs.

Natural and Everyday Drugs: A False Sense of Security 93

The pressure from society to be thin may cause teen girls to be upset with the person they see in the mirror. Some girls will turn to herbal supplements to try to lose weight.

Ginseng is one herb that is used as a weight loss supplement. However, studies show that products like this do little or nothing to aid in weight loss.

- 6.8 times more likely to have ever used methamphetamines.
- 8.1 times more likely to have ever used IV drugs.
- 8.8 times more likely to have ever used heroin.
- 14.5 times more likely to have ever used steroids.

Overall, 28.6 percent of teens reported using herbal products. Herbal product use increased with age (25 percent of ninth graders to 30 percent of twelfth graders) and varied by ethnicity (33 percent of Hispanics, 31 percent of Caucasians, 29 percent of Asians, Native Americans, or Pacific Islanders, and 12 percent of African Americans), but not by gender.

However, Dr. Yussman also cautioned against directly linking herbal product use with drug use: "This was a

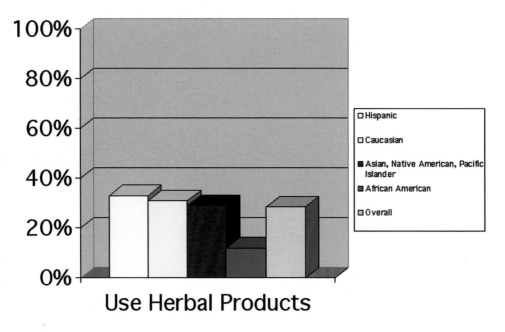

□ Hispanic	
□ Caucasian	
■ Asian, Native American, Pacific Islander	
■ African American	
□ Overall	

Use Herbal Products

Overall, 28.6% of teens reported using herbal products. Product use does seem to vary by ethnicity, but there is no difference between the percentage of males and females using herbal products.

cross-sectional study that examines an association, not a **causal link**." Dr. Yussman also said further studies are needed to determine which herbal products may be associated with use of which specific drugs. "A teen using a sports-enhancing product probably has a very different substance use pattern than a teen taking Echinacea for a cold."

What About Vitamin and Mineral Supplements?

Of course the most common of everyday drugs is the one-a-day vitamin your mom nags you to take every morning. So what's wrong with that?

Absolutely nothing, particularly given the poor nutritional habits many teens have. Still, however, the best

Experts warn about making assumptions about drug use. There should not be the same concern about a teen taking echinacea for his cold as there would be about an athlete looking to enhance her performance.

Natural and Everyday Drugs: A False Sense of Security 97

Many teens take a one-a-day multivitamin, which is fine. Of course, it would be better to get those vitamins from a healthy diet including lots of fruits and vegetables.

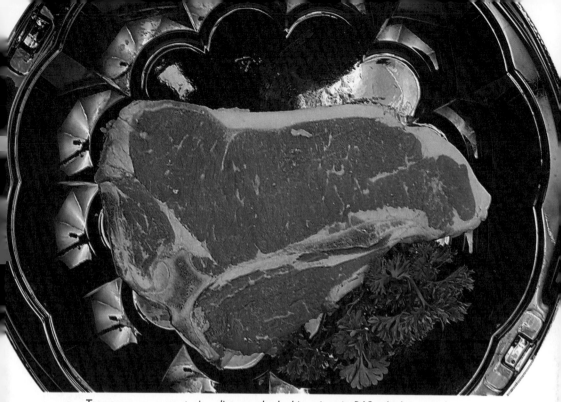

Teenagers on a vegetarian diet may be lacking vitamin B12, which is mainly found in animal products. Therefore, a supplement might be necessary to replace this missing part of their diet.

way to get your daily dose of vitamins and minerals is from food. Although there's usually nothing wrong with a teen taking a basic multivitamin, if you're eating well, you probably don't need one. If you do choose to take a multivitamin, stick with a basic supplement and avoid brands that contain higher doses than 100 percent of the recommended daily allowance for any vitamin or mineral. When taken in excess amounts, some vitamins can build up in the body and cause problems.

Talk to your doctor about additional vitamin and mineral supplements. If you can't eat dairy products, for example, you might need a calcium supplement. Vegetarians might want to take vitamin B12 (a vitamin that is found mainly in food that comes from animals and may be missing in a vegetarian diet). Teens whose doctors have

It is important to discuss dietary needs, such as vitamins and minerals, with your doctor. However, in the end, you have to decide what to put inside your own body.

put them on weight-loss diets of less than 1,200 calories a day or teens with food allergies should also discuss vitamin and mineral needs with their doctors.

In the end, choosing what to put inside your body—whether it's some form of natural or everyday drug, or something a whole lot more dangerous—is a personal choice. In other words: you're going to have to decide for yourself!

6 Making Responsible Choices

As a young adult, you're at a stage in your life where people are probably talking to you a lot about becoming "responsible." It may seem like responsibility is all about the things you have to do for other people—homework, household chores, obeying your parents' rules. Ultimately, however, especially as you grow older, responsibility is about doing what's right for *you*. Sure your parents want you to be careful when you drive; they want you to do well in school; they probably want you to have a nutritious diet and get enough sleep. And you probably want to keep your parents happy (and you should!)—but driving carefully keeps *you* safe, doing well in school helps *you* achieve your goals for the future, and taking care of your body by making wise choices will make *your* life better. So it's not so much about your parents and the other adults in your life as it is about you and what is best for *you*.

Responsibility has to do with making choices and accepting the consequences of those choices. Inevitably, we all make mistakes; being responsible means we learn and grow from those mistakes.

For most teenage girls, the "perfect body" of the media is an unattainable myth. However, exercise is a healthier way than herbal supplements to make the most of the body you have.

The Advocates for Youth website offers these ways to build a greater sense of responsibility and appreciation for the human body:

1. Encourage positive comments and try to avoid negative comments about your own and other people's bodies.

2. Participate in physical activities that make you feel good about yourself without making anyone else feel bad about their body.

3. Try not to make judgmental comments about food, calories, dieting, and weight. People of all sizes have issues around these and you never know how you will affect people with your comments.

4. Learn the facts and challenge the myths on size and bodies.

5. Compliment people more often on their ideas, personality, and accomplishments than on their appearance and physical being.

6. Try to think of bodies as whole, functional units, rather than breaking them down into parts. Instead of saying "I'm unhappy with my thighs," say, "I'm pleased that my body is capable of doing this activity well."

7. Don't participate in, encourage, or laugh at jokes that make fun of a person's body.

8. Accept all types of bodies as beautiful and challenge limiting societal standards of beauty.

9. Wear the clothes that you like and feel comfortable in, rather than what you think makes you look "too fat" or "too thin."

10. Try to eat when you are hungry, enjoy your food, and take pleasure in the process of eating, without guilt or stress over what you are eating.

11. Object to gender-based assumptions on how bodies should look, such as "women should be thin" or "men should be muscular."

12. Don't endanger your body's strength by taking products that could damage your body or diminish its abilities in some way.

Are Most Teenagers Responsible?

Adolescents often have a bad reputation for making foolish choices, for not being responsible. The research indicates, however, that more and more young adults are acting more responsibly by avoiding tobacco, marijuana, risky sexual behavior, and other potentially dangerous behaviors that increase their risk for injury, illness and death. A report from the Centers for Disease Control and Prevention (CDC), based on surveys of ninth- to twelfth-grade students in 2009, also showed teenagers are more likely today to wear seatbelts and stay out of cars with drivers who have been drinking.

Teens are often misrepresented as always making the wrong choice. However, recent surveys indicate that teens are making smart decisions, like staying out of cars driven by someone who has been drinking.

Your parents want what is best for you. However, when you make responsible choices, you should be doing it for your successful future, not just to make your parents happy.

Natural and Everyday Drugs: A False Sense of Security

According to the CDC, many high school students are making responsible choices. However, a large percentage of teens continue to engage in risky behaviors.

Underage drinking at parties is still a problem. Besides the dangers posed by alcohol itself, drinking inhibits a teen's ability to make smart decisions about other things, such as sexual encounters. .

According to an official at the CDC, "The youth in our high schools are increasingly acting like responsible young men and women—making responsible choices that will protect themselves now and well into the future." That's the good news. But there's bad news too: a significant percentage of young adults are still engaging in risky behaviors.

The 2009 report is a part of the Youth Risk Behavior Surveillance System, which monitors six areas of priority health-risk behaviors among youth, including behaviors that lead to unintentional injuries and violence, tobacco use, alcohol and other drug use, sexual behaviors, dietary behaviors and physical activity. The report includes data

The Youth Risk Behavior Surveillance System monitors risky behaviors among youth across the United States. The most recent research indicates that there is a decrease in risky sexual behaviors.

for the nation and for 34 states and 18 large cities. Here are the results of the research:

> Positive trends in most measures of students' injury- and violence-related behaviors, as well as sexual behaviors that increase the risk for HIV infection, other STDs, and unintended pregnancies. In a few areas, the trends go the other way—including a significant drop since 1991 in the percentage of students who receive daily

Physical education used to be a requirement in most high schools. However, fewer schools offer it today, which puts more teens at risk of obesity and its associated illnesses.

Natural and Everyday Drugs: A False Sense of Security

physical education instruction—increasing their risks of obesity and related illnesses. Injury- and violence-related behaviors that showed a continued decrease since they were first examined in the

Another positive trend shows that, since the early 1990s, the number of teens who do not regularly wear seatbelts has decreased from 26% to 14%.

The number of teens who smoke has been decreasing since the 1990s. Many teens are making smarter choices about cigarettes.

early '90s include the percentage of students who never or rarely wore seatbelts (26 percent to 9.7 percent); rode with a driver who had been drinking alcohol (40 percent to 28.3 percent); seriously considered suicide (29 percent to 13.8 percent); or attempted suicide (19 percent to 6.3 percent). In addition, the percentage of students who carried a weapon remained constant from 1997–2001 (18 percent to 17 percent), and then decreased from 2001–2009 (17 percent to 5.6 percent). The percentage of students who reported current cigarette use increased from 1991–1997 (28 percent to 36 percent), decreased (29 percent between 1997 and 2001), and then decreased again from 2001

Students are being smarter about sex. The percentage of students who are sexually active has decreased, but among those who are sexually active, condom use has increased.

114 Chapter 6—Making Responsible Choices

to 2009 to 19.5 percent. Similarly, the percentage of students who reported lifetime and current marijuana use increased from 1991–1997 (31 percent to 47 percent for lifetime use, and 15 percent to 26 percent for current use) and then decreased to 36.8 percent for lifetime use and 20.8 percent for current use by 2009. Current cocaine use increased from 1991–2001 (2 percent to 4 percent), but decreased from 2001–2009 (4 percent to 2.8 percent). The percentage of students who ever had sexual intercourse decreased from 54 percent to 46 percent from 1991–2009, and those who had four or more sexual partners decreased from 19 percent to 13.8 percent. Simultaneously, the percentage of sexually active students who used a condom at last sexual intercourse increased from 1991–2009 (46 percent to 61.1 percent). 15.8 percent of students surveyed were overweight, and twelve percent were obese. Less than one-quarter of high school students (22.3 percent) ate the recommended daily five servings of fruits and vegetables. Only 18.4 percent of students were physically active at least 60 minutes per day in the week before the survey.

Taking Care of You

In the end, this all comes down to taking care of yourself. When you were a kid, your parents took care of you—but as you become an adult, that job becomes yours. The body you have now is the only one you'll ever have. Right now you may take it for granted—or you may not particularly like your body because you feel it doesn't measure up in some way.

Our culture has created a set of unrealistic standards for human bodies. Everywhere we turn, we're bombarded by messages that we have to look a certain way, be shaped a certain way, or be able to move a certain way. It's easy to buy into these messages. But no matter whether you're a jock or a wimp, overweight or thin, beautiful or ordinary—or like most of us, somewhere in the middle of all these spectrums—your body is an amazing tool with wonderful abilities. So it pays to take care of it.

In an interview with Advocates for Youth, author Hanne Black had this to say about appreciating your body:

> I find that there's a lot of strength and a lot of self-esteem that comes from being confident that your body can do certain things and do them well. One of the best things is to figure out a couple of activities that your body does really well with and that your body is able to do. For me, for instance I am not fast, but I have an immense amount of stamina. I can walk and keep going, I can carry boxes of books all day and I can do slow, moderate-type stuff all day long and be just fine. For me, knowing that I can do that, and doing that kind of activity, really increases my confidence in my body because I know that my body is very dependable in doing that. . . . I think that that is really, really important that you can have trust and faith in your body and its abilities and you know what it can do and you know what it can do for you. It's more important for me to know that I can swim a mile than it is that I can't run fast. I get a lot of satisfaction out of

Very few people are amazing athletes or beautiful and thin; most of us fall somewhere in the middle. No matter where you fall, take care of your body because it is the only one you get.

Natural and Everyday Drugs: A False Sense of Security

Don't believe everything you read or see on the TV and be wary of products that promise miracles. Make informed, responsible choices that will help you lead a happy, healthy life.

knowing that I can depend on my body to do that and do it really well.

If you value your body for all it can do—rather than if it conforms to some make-believe standard for beauty or strength—you'll be more apt to take care of it. This means you'll think about the things you put inside your body—even when it comes to something as seemingly harmless as natural and everyday drugs like dietary supplements and caffeine. Find out the facts. Do your research. Don't just assume that because something is available that it's safe or good for you.

Get to know your body. Pay attention to how it reacts. How do you really feel after you've had a couple of cups of coffee or colas? Do you like this feeling? Keeping a journal of how you feel (just a notebook where you jot down the date, the time, how you feel, what you ate, drank, or took) can help you become more aware of your body's responses.

Be a cynical consumer: don't believe all the ads you read for miraculous natural products that will cure whatever ails you (whether it's a cold or a some extra pounds). Become comfortable talking with your doctor; that's part of being an adult, and she can help you become more aware of what your body needs to feel good. Use the Internet wisely; it's an incredible source of information on every topic under the sun, but you shouldn't believe everything out there. Check out the sites; learn to rely on reputable, scientific research rather than "true" stories posted on a website.

Bottom line: don't just go with the flow, allowing your peers and the culture in which you live to tell you how to think, behave, and look. Think about what you consume and how you live. Be responsible—to yourself!

What should you do if you want to cut down on your caffeine intake?

Most people are successful when they cut down their caffeine intake at the rate of a half a cup a day. In other words, if you're currently drinking four cups of coffee and three colas a day, cut back first to three and a half cups of coffee; next week, drop an entire cup of coffee out of your day; the week after that, try leaving a half of one of your sodas in the can; by the next week, you should be down to three coffees and two colas. Take small steps, rather than going "cold turkey." This is known as "caffeine fading."

If you choose to quit cold turkey instead, chances are you're going to experience withdrawal symptoms. People who cut their caffeine intake suddenly often report being irritable, distractible, nervous, restless, and feeling sleepy, as well as having a headache. In extreme cases, nausea and vomiting has also been reported. These symptoms can often be controlled with plenty of sleep and exercise—but if you're experiencing too much discomfort, you should probably instead use the caffeine-fading approach described above.

Glossary

analgesics: Medications that reduce or eliminate pain.

biochemical: Referring to processes within living organisms that involve chemical reactions.

cardiac arrhythmia: When muscles in the heart contract at an abnormal or irregular rate.

causal link: A relationship that shows one thing to be the direct cause of another.

circadian rhythm: A daily cycle of biological activity based on a twenty-four–hour period and influenced by regular variations in the environment, such as the alternation of night and day.

clinical: Based on actual observation and treatment of patients, rather than on experimentation or theory.

compound: A substance composed of two or more elements, whose composition does not change (such as water, which is made up of hydrogen and oxygen).

cross-sectional study: A method of study that observes variables in some portion of a population all at the same time, giving a "snapshot" of the effect of those variables at one point in time.

hallucinogenic: A substance that causes the user to hallucinate, to see or hear things that are not really there.

in vitro: A biological process made to occur in a laboratory vessel, or someplace other than within a living organism.

mate: A highly caffeinated drink prepared by steeping dried leaves of yerba mate (*Ilex paraguariensis*) in hot water. It is the national drink in Uruguay and Argentina, and drinking mate is a common social practice in Paraguay and parts of Chile and Brazil.

psychomotor: Pertaining to actions, or movements that are the result of mental activity.

puberty: The stage of life when an individual becomes physically capable of sexual reproduction, marked by maturing of the genital organs, development of secondary sex characteristics, and the first occurrence of menstruation in the female.

stimulant: A drug, such as caffeine, that causes increased activity, especially of the nervous or cardiovascular systems.

tachycardia: An excessively rapid heartbeat.

testimonials: Statements given to support the claims about a product, such as "I lost 60 pounds using this amazing product."

Further Reading

Cherniske, Steven. *Caffeine Blues: Wake Up to the Hidden Dangers of America's #1 Drug*. New York: Warner Books, 2005.

Clayton, Lawrence. *Diet Pill Drug Dangers*. Berkeley Heights, N.J.: Enslow, 2000.

Fillon, Mike. *Conquering Caffeine Dependence: Natural Approaches to Reducing Caffeine Intake*. Orem, Ut.: Woodland Publishing, 2001.

Harkness, Richard and Steven Bratman. *The Natural Pharmacist: Drug-Herb-Vitamin Interactions Bible*. Rocklin, Calif.: Prima Lifestyles, 2001.

Kaur, Navleen. *The Truth About Caffeine: How Companies That Promote It Deceive Us and What We Can Do About It*. New York: SCR Books, 2006.

Monroe, Judy. *Herbal Drug Dangers*. Berkeley Heights, N.J.: Enslow, 2001.

For More Information

Family Education
life.familyeducation.com/nutrition/foods/36515.html

Kids' Health
www.kidshealth.org/teen/ food_fitness/nutrition.html

Mercy Medical Center Resources
healthychoice.epnet.com/getcontent.asp?SiteID=mmc

NIDA for Teens
teens.drugabuse.gov

TeenGrowth.com
www.teengrowth.com/index.cfm?action=info_advice&ID_Advice=1227

The websites listed on this page were active at the time of publication. The publisher is not responsible for websites that have changed their addresses or discontinued operation since the date of publication. The publisher will review and update the website list upon each reprint.

Bibliography

Cherniske, Steven. *Caffeine Blues: Wake Up to the Hidden Dangers of America's #1 Drug*. New York: Warner Books, 2005.

DeSmet, A.S.M. "Herbal Remedies," *New England Journal Medicine* 347, 25:2046–56, 2002.

Dietary Supplement Enforcement Report. www.fda.gov/oc/nutritioninitiative/report.html

"FDA Announces Initiative to Provide Better Health Information for Consumers." www.fda.gov/bbs/topics/NEWS/2002/NEW00859.html

Fillon, Mike. *Conquering Caffeine Dependence: Natural Approaches to Reducing Caffeine Intake*. Orem, Ut.: Woodland Publishing, 2001.

Kaur, Navleen. *The Truth About Caffeine: How Companies That Promote It Deceive Us and What We Can Do About It*. New York: SCR Books, 2006.

Marcus, D. and A. Grollman. "Botanical Medicines: The Need for New Regulations," *New England Journal Medicine* 347, 25:2073–6, 2002.

"Natural Drugs." http://www.kidshealth.org/teen/nutrition/weight/diet_supplements.html

Straus, Stephen. "Herbal Medicines: What's in the Bottle?" *New England Journal Medicine* 347, 25:1997–8, 2002.

U. S. Department of Health and Human Services, U.S. Food & Drug Administration, Center for Food Safety & Applied Nutrition. "Dietary Supplements." http://vm.cfsan.fda.gov/~dms/supplmnt.html

Index

Picture Credits

Comstock 12
Drug Enforcement Agency (DEA) 88
GNU Free Documentation License 86, 92
Elisseeva, Elena 108
Eric Hunt 86
Image Source 67
istock.com 17, 21, 22, 52, 60, 62, 81, 82
    Christine Balderas 52
    Robert Churchill 22
    David Crockett 13
    Lise Gagne 82
    Nikolai Okhitin 21
    Nick Schlax 66
    Susan Trigg 81
Jägenstedt, Philip 10
Jupiter Images 8, 13, 14, 25, 28, 31, 32, 39, 40, 42, 45, 47, 48, 49, 50, 54, 55, 56, 57, 58, 59, 65, 68, 71, 72, 73, 74, 75, 76, 77, 79, 80, 81, 94, 97, 98, 99, 100, 102, 104, 106, 107, 109, 110, 111, 112, 113, 114, 117, 118
Photolink, 34
S. Solum/Photolink 18
USDA/Agricultural Research Service 91
Vlue 76

To the best knowledge of the publisher, all other images are in the public domain. If any image has been inadvertently uncredited, please notify Harding House Publishing Services, Vestal, New York 13850, so that rectification can be made for future printings.

Author and Consultant Biographies

Author

Ida Walker, the author of many nonfiction books for young adults, lives in New York State.

Series Consultant

Jack E. Henningfield, Ph.D., is a professor at the Johns Hopkins University School of Medicine, and he is also Vice President for Research and Health Policy at Pinney Associates, a consulting firm in Bethesda, Maryland, that specializes in science policy and regulatory issues concerning public health, medications development, and behavior-focused disease management. Dr. Henningfield has contributed information relating to addiction to numerous reports of the U.S. Surgeon General, the National Academy of Sciences, and the World Health Organization.